Jackrabbits

By JoAnn Early Macken

Reading Consultant: Jeanne Clidas, Ph.D.
Director, Roberts Wesleyan College Literacy Clinic

WEEKLY READER®
PUBLISHING

Please visit our web site at **www.garethstevens.com**.
For a free catalog describing our list of high-quality books,
call 1-877-542-2595 (USA) or 1-800-387-3178 (Canada).
Our fax: 1-877-542-2596

Library of Congress Cataloging-in-Publication Data

Macken, JoAnn Early, 1953–
      Jackrabbits / by JoAnn Early Macken; reading consultant, Jeanne Clidas.
         p. cm. — (Animals that live in the desert)
      Includes bibliographical references and index.
      ISBN-10: 1-4339-2194-4   ISBN-13: 978-1-4339-2194-0 (lib. bdg.)
      ISBN-10: 1-4339-2450-1   ISBN-13: 978-1-4339-2450-7 (soft cover)
      1. Jackrabbits—Juvenile literature. I. Title.
QL737.L32M333   2010
599.32'8—dc22
                                        2009002867

This edition first published in 2010 by
Weekly Reader® Books
An Imprint of Gareth Stevens Publishing
1 Reader's Digest Road
Pleasantville, NY 10570-7000 USA

Executive Managing Editor: Lisa M. Herrington
Senior Editor: Barbara Bakowski
Project Management: Spooky Cheetah Press
Cover Designers: Jennifer Ryder-Talbot and Studio Montage
Production: Studio Montage
Library Consultant: Carl Harvey, Library Media Specialist, Noblesville, Indiana

Photo credits: Cover, pp. 1, 15 Shutterstock; p. 5 © James P. Rowan; p. 7 © Rick and Nora Bowers/Visuals Unlimited
p. 9 © Richard Day/Daybreak Imagery; p. 11 © Corel; p. 13 ©Tom and Pat Leeson; p. 17 © Michael H. Francis;
p. 19 © Jeff Foott/naturepl.com; p. 21 © John and Barbara Gerlach/Visuals Unlimited

Printed in the United States of America

1 2 3 4 5 6 7 8 9 14 13 12 11 10 09

Table of Contents

Boldface words appear in the glossary.

Desert Hare

Jackrabbits are hares. Hares are longer and thinner than rabbits. They have long, strong **hind** legs.

hind leg

In hot weather, jackrabbits lift their long ears to cool off. In cold weather, they keep their ears down to stay warm. They can turn their ears to hear better.

ears

Jackrabbits are gray, brown, and white. Their colors blend into the dry **desert**.

Some jackrabbits have black tips on their ears. They have a black stripe on their tails.

tail

Jackrabbits are active at night. They eat grass, twigs, and desert plants.

Staying Safe

Jackrabbits eat in open areas. They watch out for hawks, owls, and coyotes.

Jackrabbits run fast to get away from **predators**. They leap on their long, strong legs.

During the day, jackrabbits rest in the shade. They may rest under a bush or a **cactus**. They may rest in shallow holes they dig in the ground.

cactus

Baby Jackrabbits

Baby jackrabbits are born with soft fur. Their eyes are open. Their mother feeds them milk at first. In about one month, they can be on their own.

Fast Facts

Length	about 2 feet (61 centimeters)
Weight	about 9 pounds (4 kilograms)
Diet	grasses and desert plants
Average life span	up to 5 years

Glossary

cactus: a desert plant with a thick stem and spiny leaves

desert: a dry area with little rainfall

hind: back

predators: animals that kill and eat other animals

For More Information

Books

Jackrabbit's Tale. Soundprints Read-and-Discover (series). Trish Kline. (Little Soundprints, 2002)

Jackrabbits. Emily Rose Townsend (Pebble Books, 2003)

Web Sites

Jackrabbit

animals.nationalgeographic.com/animals/mammals/ jackrabbit.html
Read a jackrabbit profile. Print out your own fact sheet.

Jackrabbits

www.desertusa.com/july96/du_rabbi.html
Watch a video of desert rabbits.

Index

About the Author

JoAnn Early Macken is the author of two rhyming picture books, *Sing-Along Song* and *Cats on Judy*, and more than 80 nonfiction books for children. Her poems have appeared in several children's magazines. She lives in Wisconsin with her husband and their two sons.